Contents

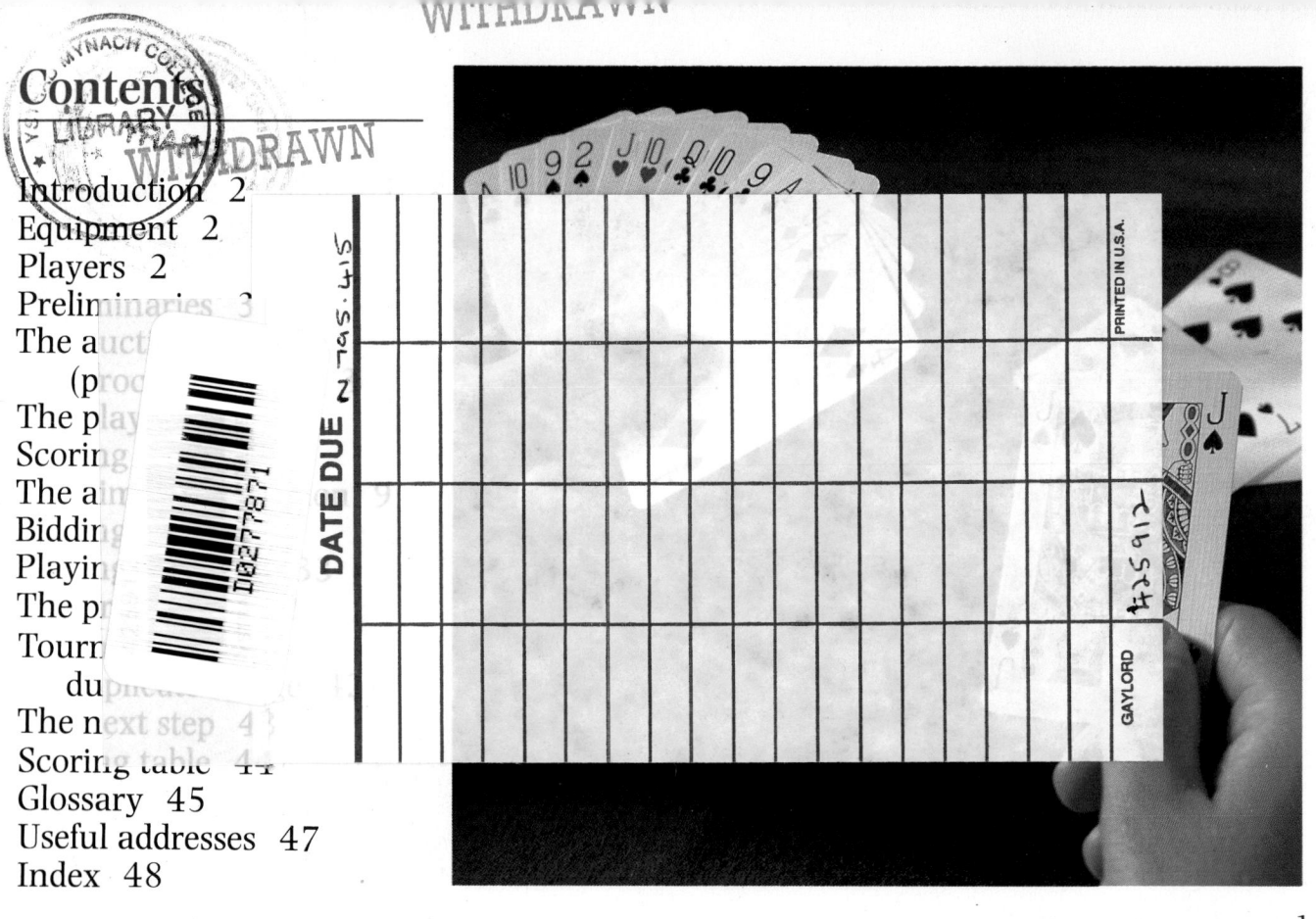

Introduction

Bridge is one of the most interesting and popular games in the world. The object of this book is to enable you to acquire a thorough knowledge of both the rules and the fundamentals, so that when you take your place at the bridge table you will be able to hold your own in modest company.

Acknowledgements
Text by T. E. Bramley.
The publishers would like to thank Waddingtons for their contribution to this book.

Photography by Mike Ellis.

Note Throughout the book bridge players are referred to individually as 'he'. This should, of course, be taken to mean 'he or she' where appropriate.

Equipment

Two packs of cards are used. A pack consists of 52 cards with 13 cards in each of the four suits. The suits rank downwards in scoring value in the following order: spades, hearts, diamonds, clubs. The cards of each suit rank downwards in playing and scoring order: ace, king, queen, jack, 10, 9, 8, 7, 6, 5, 4, 3, 2. Each player should have a scoring pad and pencil. The pad is divided into vertical columns, alternately headed 'WE' and 'THEY'. In the WE column you put your own scores, and in the THEY column your opponents' scores.

Players

Bridge is a game for four players: North and South play as partners against East and West. A pack of cards is spread face downwards on the table and the players each select a card. The two players drawing the two highest cards play together. If cards of the same rank are drawn, the value of the suit determines the highest.

The player drawing the highest card deals first. He has the right to choose his seat and the pack of cards with which he will deal. His partner faces him and the opponents choose their seats on his left and right.

Preliminaries

The shuffle and the cut

After the first dealer has chosen one of the packs, the player on his left shuffles the cards. The dealer then passes the pack to the player on his right for him to cut. This is done by lifting a portion from the top and placing it beside the bottom portion. The dealer then completes the cut by placing the bottom portion on the top one. Each portion must contain at least four cards.

While the deal is in progress the dealer's partner shuffles the second pack and places it face downwards on his right. This pack is not distributed until the next deal, when the new dealer hands it to his right-hand opponent for him to cut. He may shuffle it himself, however, before handing it over to be cut.

Shuffling must be carried out thoroughly and in full view of all the players, but without exposing any card.

If any card is exposed during the cutting, or if for any other reason there is a re-deal, the cards must be re-shuffled and re-cut. Only the dealer may re-shuffle the cards.

The deal

The dealer deals the cards face downwards, one at a time, starting with the player on his left and continuing clockwise round the table. Each player will receive 13 cards, and the last card will be dealt to the dealer himself.

No card must be exposed during the deal and no player may look at a card until the deal is completed.

After the first hand has been played the deal passes to the next player on the left. Thus if North deals first, East will be the second dealer, South the third and West the fourth, and so on until the end of the rubber, unless there is a re-deal of any hand when the dealer re-deals.

Re-deals must take place if:

● the cards are not dealt correctly, or a card is exposed during the deal
● an incorrect number of cards is dealt to any player.

The auction (procedure only)

When the last card has been dealt the players pick up their cards and sort them into suits with the cards in the order of importance in each suit.

Beginning with the dealer, each player in rotation now has the chance to call and can choose one of four alternatives: **pass**, **double** or **re-double** (the two latter terms are explained on page 7). An initial pass signifies that the player does not have an opening bid. A **bid** contracts to win a specified number of tricks in a named suit or in no-trumps. There are five possible denominations in which the contract may be selected. In order of precedence they are:

● no-trumps
● spades
● hearts
● diamonds
● clubs.

The first six tricks scored by a partnership are known as the **book** and they do not count towards the score. Any tricks made in addition to the book are known as **odd** tricks. When a player bids one no-trump or one of a suit, he says that he is prepared to make a total of seven tricks, or one over the book. The highest possible bid is seven, which is a contract to win all 13 tricks.

A condition of any bid is that it must be higher than the preceding bid. It must name a greater number of odd tricks or the same number of odd tricks but in a higher ranking suit. For example, a bid of three no-trumps is higher than a bid of three of any other suit but it may be overruled by a bid of four clubs or anything higher.

Each time a player's turn comes to bid he may make only one call and he cannot change that call once it is made unless he does so practically in the same breath. A call out of rotation or a change of calls is subject to penalty.

The auction continues until three players pass consecutively. If there was no bid during the auction, the hands are thrown in and the deal passes to the next player.

If any bids were made, the last bid becomes the contract. If a suit was named by the last bidder, it becomes the trump suit and the player who first named the suit is termed the **declarer** and plays the hand.

A player who does not hear a call distinctly may ask for it to be repeated because no redress is allowed in the game for a call based on a misunderstanding. A player may ask for the previous calls to be repeated when it is his turn to call or after the auction has finished if play has not started.

The play

The object of the play is to win tricks. A **trick** consists of four cards – one played by each player in rotation. The highest card played of the suit led wins the trick unless the suit has been trumped.

The defender on declarer's left makes the opening lead. He selects one of the cards from his hand and places it face upwards on the table. The declarer's partner then places all his cards, arranged into suits with the trumps on his right, face upwards in front of him on the table. This player and his hand become the **dummy**. The dummy player takes no further part in the play of the hand.

After the opening lead the declarer selects a card from dummy and places it face upwards in the centre of the table. In turn, the second defender and the declarer select a card from their hands and also place it face upwards on the table. Fig. 1 shows the order of the play. The selected cards must be of the

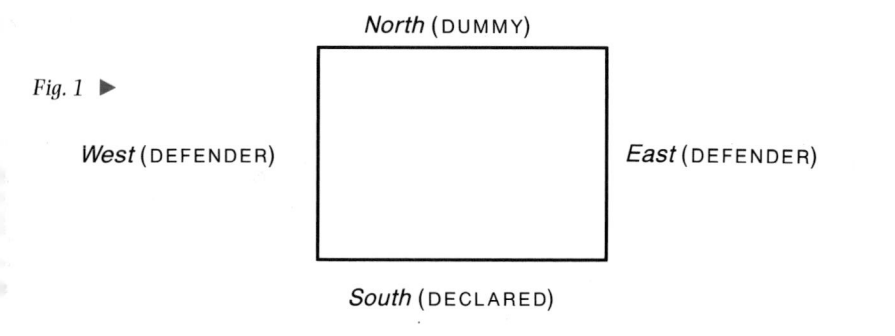

Fig. 1 ▶

North (DUMMY)

West (DEFENDER)

East (DEFENDER)

South (DECLARED)

Dummy's rights

After dummy's cards are placed on the table, dummy's rights are strictly limited. From now on dummy may not interfere during play in any way except to:

● make sure that his partner leads from the correct hand
● enquire if his partner (declarer) fails to follow in a particular suit, 'No hearts, partner?'.

However, these rights are forfeited if dummy looks at an opponent's hand. Except in the two situations mentioned, dummy should remain silent throughout.

same suit as the card which was led, but if any player does not possess a card of that suit he may play any card. Playing a card of the same suit is called **following suit**. Playing a card of the same suit is called a **discard** unless a card of the suit named in the final bid is played: this is called a **trump**.

The highest trump, or the highest card in the suit that was led, wins the trick. The player winning the trick leads to the second trick and the other players play their cards in rotation. If the trick was won by dummy, the lead to the second trick must come from dummy. The winner of the second trick leads to the third trick and so on until all 13 tricks have been won.

When the hand is finished the score is entered on the score pads and the next deal is started.

When a trick is completed the cards must be gathered and turned face downwards on the table by the side winning it. The cards of each trick should be kept together so that the trick can be identified easily. All the tricks taken by a side should be arranged together in front of the declarer or of one defender in such a manner that their number and sequence are apparent.

Scoring

The score card has a horizontal line across it. Scores entered *above* this line are for premiums and honours; scores entered *below* the line are for tricks. Premium points are entered in ascending order above the line and trick points are entered in descending order below it.

Below the line scores

Scores may only be entered below the line for contracts bid and made. Each trick has a point value according to the suit or no-trump value of the contract as shown below:

		If doubled	If re-doubled
Spades	30	60	120
Hearts	30	60	120
Diamonds	20	40	80
Clubs	20	40	80
No-trumps:			
– first trick	40	80	160
– second and subsequent tricks	30	60	120

Game scores

Only points entered *below* the line count towards game scores; the points for extra tricks go *above* the line. This is why it is very important for the declarer to bid the full value of his hand. There will be more about this later in the book.

Whenever a side gets 100 points below the line, a game is scored. A line is then drawn beneath the trick score for both sides, and the trick scores for the next game are entered below this line. Trick scores cannot be carried on from one game to the next: both sides start with no points when the line is drawn. No bonus points are scored for winning a single game. A completed score card is shown on page 8.

A 'rubber' of bridge consists of the best of three games and is finished when either side has won two games.

Above the line scores

Scores above the line can be entered for the following reasons:

- over-tricks
- honours
- bonus for making a doubled or re-doubled contract
- bonus for winning a rubber
- bonus for making a slam
- bonus for over-tricks made when doubled
- premium points for defeating the contract.

These various means of scoring above the line will now be explained. Above the line scores have no effect on a current game but they all contribute to the ultimate score made by a side.

Over-trick points

A contract of two hearts bid and made scores 60 points below the line (*see* table on page 6). A side which makes three hearts can still only enter 60 points below the line, but the 30 points for the extra trick are entered above the line. Tricks made in excess of the contract are called **over-tricks**.

Honours

The five highest cards in any suit, that is the ace, king, queen, jack and 10, are called **honour** cards. When a suit contract is played, i.e. when there is a trump suit, any player who has in his hand four of the five top trump suit cards scores 100 points for his side. If a player has all the five top honours he scores 150 points. If he has the four aces he also scores 150 points, but only when the hand is played in no-trumps.

Vulnerable and non-vulnerable scores

When either side has won a game they become **vulnerable**. A side which has not won a game is **non-vulnerable**. A vulnerable side becomes liable to extra penalties if it fails to make a contract.

Double and re-double

During the bidding it is open to any player to **double** the last bid made by an opponent. If all the other players pass, the hand is played in the doubled contract. If the contract is made – say three spades, 180 points scored – this counts as a game (although the game has not been called).

Should the contract fail the penalties are:

- **non-vulnerable**   100 for 1st under-trick
200 for 2nd and 3rd under-trick
300 for each subsequent under-trick

For example, 1 away 100, 2 away 300, 4 away 800.

- **vulnerable**   200 for 1st under-trick
300 for each subsequent under-trick

For example, 1 away 200, 2 away 500, 3 away 800.

When a contract is doubled it is open to the bidder or his partner to **re-double** if he wishes. Re-doubling doubles the premium points for over-tricks which, when doubled, are 100 points non-vulnerable and 200 when vulnerable. The doubled scores below the line are also doubled again. Thus if you are doubled and you re-double a contract of one spade, you now score 120 points and also make a game.

Bonus for a doubled or re-doubled contract

A bonus of 50 points is awarded for a doubled contract successfully made. If re-doubled the bonus is 100 points.

Bonus for winning a rubber

A rubber ends when a side has won two games. The winners of the final game add to their score 700 points if the opponents have not won a game, and 500 points if their opponents have won a game.

Bonus for slam

A contract of six odd tricks bid and made is called a **little slam**. The bonus for making this is 500 points non-vulnerable and 750 points vulnerable.

A contract of seven odd tricks bid and made is called a **grand slam**. The bonus for making a grand slam is 1000 points not vulnerable and 1,500 if vulnerable.

Adding the score

At the end of a rubber each side totals up the scores under the WE and THEY columns on the scoring pad. The trick and the premium points are added together and the side with the larger total wins, the winning margin being the difference in the scores irrespective of the number of games which either side has won.

Fig. 2 is an example of a completed score card. (This is the North-South record of the rubber.) The hand resulted as follows.

● **First hand:** North-South bid and made two hearts.

● **Second hand:** East-West bid and made two no-trumps plus one over-trick.

● **Third hand:** North-South bid and made two spades to win the first game.

● **Fourth hand:** East-West bid three hearts which was doubled by North-South and failed by three under-tricks – 500 points.

● **Fifth hand:** North-South bid and made four spades and so won the second game. North-South therefore collects 700 points for the rubber.

▲ *Fig. 2 Completed score card*

The final scores are therefore North-South 1440, East-West 100. Thus North-South won the rubber by 1340 points.

Scoring an unfinished rubber

If for any reason the rubber cannot be finished, the score is computed as follows. If only one game has been completed the winners of that game score 300 points. If one side has a part score in an unfinished game, that side scores 100 points. The trick and premium scores are added and the side with the larger total wins, the winning margin being the difference in the scores.

Summary of scoring

Scoring at bridge is complicated, and it takes a little while to learn and remember the different values of the scoring items. Although they have been explained in some detail in the preceding pages, for convenience they are summarised on page 44. Players are advised to keep a scoring summary, such as this, by their side when playing until such time as they have memorised the table.

The aim of the auction

The aim of the bidding is to reach a contract which can be fulfilled exactly. Sometimes a player will get a good hand based on a trick-taking valuation; sometimes he will get a hand incapable of taking a trick. Usually he will get a hand with obvious potentialities for taking one or two tricks. Bidding should aim at getting a contract of the full value of the hand, unless the side concerned already has a part scored. In this case it is only necessary to bid sufficient to complete the game.

The table of scores emphasises the need to bid to the full value of the hand. Over-tricks count nothing towards the game score. Under-bidding can be costly. The declaring side may fail to reach a game contract which is there, and on the very next deal opponents can bid and make the rubber.

A non-vulnerable side loses 50 points for each under-trick; a vulnerable side loses 100 points. If the contract is doubled the penalties are considerably higher.

In the majority of hands over-bidding can hardly be excused, although 'sacrifice bidding' is an accepted part of the game. Suppose both sides are vulnerable; the side to win the next game will score 500 points for the rubber. But if one side were to bid four hearts and the other to bid four spades (though they could reasonably expect to make only nine tricks) the latter would only lose 200 points as against 620 for the game and rubber.

How then does a side bid to a contract which they can fulfil and at the same time encourage their opponents to bid a contract beyond their attainments? It is obvious that a player must get some idea of how many tricks he can make with his partner's help. This is done by valuing his own hand before the auction starts and then by a 'one-over-one' method of bidding to reach the best contract.

Valuation of the hand

Many systems for valuing the hand have been invented and developed. Some are very difficult and complicated. At the beginning of a game of bridge each side is entitled to ask their opponents what system they are playing. It is better to play a simple system, and the one described below is best for the beginner.

In this system the high cards are given a point value:

- ace: 4 points
- king: 3 points
- queen: 2 points
- jack: 1 point.

In the pack there are 52 cards which include four aces, four kings, four queens and four jacks. The maximum number of points for high cards, therefore, is 40. If each player were dealt an average hand, he would have a point count of ten.

There are, of course, other trick-winning cards. Low cards can easily win tricks if they are played as trumps, but in order to be able to play a trump the player must not have any cards in the suit led.

An average deal would give a player three cards in each of three suits and four in the remaining one. Should he be dealt a hand with an unbalanced distribution he may, once play has started, be in a position to use one or more of his small trumps to make tricks.

When a player is dealt a hand which contains no cards of a suit, he has what is called a **void suit**; if the hand contains only one card of a suit, that card is called a **singleton**; while if the hand has two cards in a suit, that suit becomes a **doubleton**. All such suits are called short suits.

Number of cards in each suit:

	(♠)	(♥)	(♦)	(♣)	Remarks
1st deal	6	4	Nil	3	Void suit in diamonds
2nd deal	3	6	1	3	Singleton in diamonds
3rd deal	2	4	4	3	Doubleton in spades

It should be remembered that the point count is not an exact indication but merely a useful guide, especially for no-trump bidding. 25 points are usually enough for a game in no-trumps, but this must not be applied too rigidly where a suit contract is concerned. In this case the most important thing is the distribution of the hand, and a game in a suit contract may be made with far fewer than 25 points if the hand contains a long trump suit with a singleton, doubleton or void in either hand.

No. of points in the combined hands	Possible contract (based on hands of even distribution)	No. of odd tricks
Less than 20	None	Nil
20–24	Part score	1–3
25 or more	Game	3–5
33 or more	Little slam	6
37 or more	Grand slam	7

With a point count of less than 20, the opponents will probably play the hand. With a point count of 21–24, and with a balanced distribution, the best that you can hope for is a part score. With 25 or over it should be possible to make a game.

The next step is to convey the strength of your hand to your partner and to learn his strength – and also that of your opponents.

Bidding

The first player to bid in the auction is called the **opening bidder**. When should a player make an opening bid? Obviously when he has more than his share of high cards.

Opening bids can be made on the point values in Table A opposite.

When it is the partner's turn to bid he becomes the **responder**. The nature of his response will be described later, but for the present only his point valuation need be considered. The support that he can give his partner is shown in Table B.

In the absence of any other information, the responder must assume that the opening bidder has no more than 13 points and make his response accordingly. The further development of the bidding will give both opener and responder a better idea of the strength of each other's hand, and lead to the fixing of the final contract.

The opponents are likely to take part in the bidding, but this can help to determine where the high cards are placed.

Point value of the hand	Call
12 points or fewer	Pass
13 points	Optional opening which depends on whether you are able to make your second bid
14 points or over	A bid must be made

▲ *Table A*

Point value of opening bid	Point value held by responder	Point value of combined hands	Contract points
13	Fewer than 6	Fewer than 19	No contract
13	Up to 11	19 to 24	Part score
13	12 to 16	25 to 29	Game
13	17 or more	30 or more	Game (possibility of slam)

▲ *Table B*

Opening bids

It is possible to bid a suit or, alternatively, to bid in no-trumps. We will deal first with bidding in a suit.

One of a suit

Let us suppose that having valued your hand you find that it is worth 13 points, and you decide to make an opening bid. You are not allowed to say to the others: 'I have a point count of 13 and some good cards in hearts. What have you got, partner?' But you can say: 'One heart.'

The opening bidder must have in his hand a biddable or a rebiddable suit. The purpose in bidding a suit is to suggest it as a trump suit. For that purpose it must contain four or more cards headed by one or more honours. The possible biddable suits containing four cards above a jack are shown below.

- A K Q J   A Q x x   K Q x x
- A K Q x   A J x x   K J x x
- A K J x   A x x x   K x x x
- A K x x   K Q J x   Q J x x

A five-card or longer suit is biddable whether it has high cards or not. The strength of such a suit lies in its length.

Re-biddable suits

A re-biddable suit is one of such strength that it can be bid again by the same player later in the auction. The first requirement is that it must contain at least five cards. Examples are:

- A K x x x   A J x x x   K Q x x x
- K J 9 x x   Q J 9 x x   A K Q x x

Are there any further principles to help you decide your opening bid? You should bid the longest suit first, and, unless you have a very strong hand, you should make it a bid of one. If there are two biddable suits in the hand you should choose the higher ranking one first. Overleaf are some examples of opening bids (all at the *one* level).

Hand	Comments	Call
(a) (♠) K Q (♥) Q 5 2 (♦) A K 6 3 2 (♣) J 10 9	Point count: 15	One diamond
(b) (♠) K Q J 5 4 (♥) A 9 3 (♦) K 8 6 (♣) 5 4	Point count: 14 One re-biddable suit	One spade
(c) (♠) 8 3 (♥) A K J 5 (♦) A K Q 3 (♣) J 7 5	Point count: 18 Biddable suits in diamonds and hearts	One heart
(d) (♠) 9 3 2 (♥) K Q J 6 5 3 (♦) 8 3 (♣) 9 4	Point count: 6	Pass
(e) (♠) J 6 (♥) A K J (♦) J 9 5 4 2 (♣) K 8 6	Point count: 13 One biddable suit	One diamond
(f) (♠) A K 5 2 (♥) A K J 6 2 (♦) 7 3 (♣) 9 4	Point count: 15 The heart suit should be bid first	One heart
(g) (♠) J 8 6 3 2 (♥) A 9 2 (♦) A J 7 (♣) A Q	Point count: 16	One spade

Responses to opening bids of one of a suit

When your partner has opened the bidding with one of a suit, and your hand contains some strength, you should strive to keep the bidding alive. This gives your partner a chance to bid again, possibly under another suit in which the hand may play better. If you have nothing, you must pass. You may keep the bidding open in one of three ways:

- by bidding in no-trumps
- by raising your partner's suit
- by bidding some other suit.

To keep the bidding open with no-trumps, you should have a hand containing between six and nine points, and without adequate support in the suit bid by your partner. If your partner opens one heart you should respond one no-trump on each of the following hands.

- (♠) 10 x x   (♥) K x x
- (♠) x x x   (♥) x x x
- (♠) x x x   (♥) x x x

- (♦) J x x   (♣) Q 10 x
- (♦) A x x   (♣) Q x x
- (♦) A J x   (♣) Q x x x

To raise to two of partner's suit

For this you should have four cards in the suit bid or three to an honour, of which one should be the queen or higher card. This is called **trump support**. Even with adequate trump support, raising of partner's suit is not automatic; the hand must contain some extra values – about seven to 10 points.

If your partner opens one heart you should bid two on each of the following hands.

- (♠) J x   (♥) 10 x x x
- (♠) x x x   (♥) K J x x
- (♠) K x x   (♥) Q J x x

- (♦) Q 10 x   (♣) K J x x
- (♦) K x x   (♣) x x x
- (♦) x x   (♣) J x x x

Responses in a new suit

So far we have considered the hands where the responder has insufficient strength to make a change of suit bid. He has either passed, bid one no-trump, or raised the opening bidder's suit. There remains the third general alternative, that of bidding a new suit. This is more restrictive than making an opening bid. For instance, after an opening bid of one heart, the responder has the choice of only one spade or one no-trump if he wishes to make a bid at the one level, otherwise he must bid two clubs or two diamonds.

We have seen that a one no-trump response means a hand with six to nine points without adequate trump support, so the other hands to be examined are the ones with one spade, two clubs or two diamonds response.

A bid by the responder of one in a suit is called the **one-over-one** response; if you name a new suit at the two level you are making a **two-over-one** response. Do not do this unless you have a minimum of eight points. Here is an example of a one-over-one response.

You are the responder and your partner has opened the bidding with one heart. You hold:

(♠) K J x x
(♥) K x x
(♦) x x
(♣) x x x x

You should now bid one spade.

For a two-over-one response you obviously need a stronger hand as you are deliberately increasing the level of the contract, at the same time forcing your partner to bid again. Here is an example of a two-over-one response.

You are the responder and your partner has opened the bidding with one heart. You hold:

(♠) x x
(♥) x x x
(♦) A x x
(♣) K Q J x x

Bid two clubs.

You hold:

(♠) x x
(♥) x x x
(♦) A Q 5 4 2
(♣) K x x

Bid two diamonds.

Bidding in no-trumps

Opening bids in no-trumps should only be made with certain types of hands. A hand with long and short suits usually plays better in a suit contract. The best hands for no-trumps are those distributed 4–3–3–3 or 4–4–3–2. In determining the value of a hand for a no-trump opening bid the point count is the best guide. Only the honour cards should be counted.

There are two methods of opening one no-trump, depending whether you are playing it strong (16–18 points) or weak (12–14 points).

Responses to an opening strong one no-trump bid

The response to an opening bid of a strong one no-trump is governed by the value of the responder's hand and its distribution. The opening bidder has shown a count of 16 to 18 points, so with as few as eight points in the responder's hand a game contract may be possible.

With 10 to 15 points a game contract should be reached, and with 16 points or more a slam is possible. A balanced distribution suggests that the response should be in no-trumps, but an unbalanced distribution favours a suit response.

With fewer than eight points the response will generally be to pass, though seven or eight points in an unbalanced hand with a long biddable suit will often lead to a game contract. With eight or nine points and a

Strong one no-trump Open one no-trump with even distribution and 16–18 points.	
(a) Q J 9 K J 3 K 8 3 A Q 6 4	(b) K 10 8 6 A J A Q 7 2 K 5 4
16 points	17 points
(c) K J 8 K 10 9 K 3 2 A Q 2 5	(d) 10 9 5 2 A Q K Q J 4 A Q 8
17 points	18 points

Hand	Combined point count	Call
(a) (♠) K 10 4 (♥) Q 8 7 5 (♦) Q 9 6 3 (♣) J 9	24 to 26	Two no-trumps

Comments: partner will raise to three if he has a maximum no-trump bid.

Hand	Combined point count	Call
(b) (♠) A Q J 5 (♥) 8 7 5 (♦) 6 3 2 (♣) 9 8 4	23 to 25	Pass

Comments: less than eight points but chance of a game in a suit if partner has a maximum.

Hand	Combined point count	Call
(c) (♠) A Q 6 5 (♥) Q 7 5 (♦) K 7 3 (♣) 9 8 4	27 to 29	Three no-trumps

Comments: balanced distribution and enough points for game.

Hand	Combined point count	Call
(d) (♠) A Q 6 5 4 (♥) Q 7 5 (♦) K 7 (♣) 9 8 4	27 to 29	Three spades

Comments: the bid indicates strength but with an unbalanced distribution.

Hand	Combined point count	Call
(e) (♠) A Q 6 5 4 (♥) Q J 5 (♦) K 7 (♣) A J 4	33 to 35	Three spades

Comments: great strength, though unbalanced. After partner has replied three no-trumps or four spades, follow this with the Blackwood Convention (*see* page 32).

balanced hand the response should be two no-trumps. With 10 to 15 points and a balanced hand, respond three no-trumps.

Partner has opened the bidding with one no-trump (strong). What is the response holding?

Weak one no-trump

The basic requirements for opening one no-trump weak are the same as for opening one no-trump strong, except that the value of the hand is 12–14 points.

Here are four examples of a weak no-trump opening.

(a) Q J 9 K J 3 K 8 5 K 9 6 2	(b) Q 10 2 Q 10 6 4 A J 2 Q J 3
13 points	12 points
(c) A 6 4 K 10 2 Q 9 8 2 A J 8	(d) J 10 4 Q 9 8 K 8 A Q J 7 4
14 points	13 points

Responses to an opening weak one no-trump bid

The opening bidder has shown a count of 12–14 points, so with values of up to 10 points a game is most unlikely. Pass.

With 11–12 points, the two hands combined may have enough strength – 25 points to be in a game contract – bid two trumps. Partner will bid three no-trumps with 14 points, or with a good 13-point count.

With more than 13 points bid three no-trumps; the combined strengths of the two hands is enough for a game contract.

Partner has opened the bidding with one no-trump, 12–14 points. What is the response holding?

Hand	Combined point count	Call
(a) (♠) K 10 4 (♥) Q 8 7 5 (♦) Q 9 6 3 (♣) J 9	20 to 22	Pass
(b) (♠) K Q 2 (♥) J 6 4 (♦) K 9 6 4 (♣) Q 10 2	23 to 25	Two no-trumps

Comments: partner will raise to three no-trumps with 14 or a good 13-point count.

Hand	Combined point count	Call
(c) (♠) A 9 6 (♥) Q 4 2 (♦) K Q 9 4 (♣) Q 10 2	25 to 27	Three no-trumps

Comments: partner will pass.

Hand	Combined point count	Call
(d) (♠) A Q J 5 4 (♥) 8 7 5 (♦) 6 3 (♣) 9 8 4	19 to 21	Two spades

Comments: a weak bid, partner should pass. The hand then plays in your best suit.

Hand	Combined point count	Call
(e) (♠) Q J 5 4 (♥) A 2 (♦) 6 4 2 (♣) Q J 10	26 to 28	Three spades

Comments: a strong bid, partner should call three no-trumps or four spades depending on his spade holding.

Weak take-out

Opposite partner's weak one no-trump opening, a poor hand can become more useful if it holds a suit of at least five cards which become trumps. With: Qxxxx, 10xx, KJx, xx bid spades; the contract of two spades is more likely to succeed than one no-trump, for your small trumps will bring in extra tricks. Your poor hand has become much better and your partner will not bid again.

After partner's one no-trump with:

x x   10 9 x   K Q 10 6 4 2 xx   xx

...bid two diamonds. After partner's one no-trump with:

K x   Q J 8 6 2   x x x   J x x

...bid two hearts. After partner's one no-trump with:

10 8 6 4 3 2   x x   x x   A x x

...bid two spades.

Openings of two no-trumps and three no-trumps and responses are not altered when playing the weak one no-trump opening.

The Stayman Convention

This is a convention designed to be used in response to an opening one no-trump bid in order to explore the possibility of playing the hand in a major suit (i.e. hearts or spades), of which the partners hold at least four cards each in that suit.

This convention entails an artificial response of two clubs to an opening one no-trump bid. The two-club bid says to your partner: 'If you have a four-card major suit headed by the jack or better, or a five-card major suit, please bid it. If not, bid two diamonds and leave the next bid to me.'

The two-club bid is a forcing bid and partner will respond with either two diamonds with no major suit, or with two hearts or two spades if he has four or more. If he holds four of each major suit he will respond with the lower ranking one, i.e. hearts.

Here is an example of the Stayman Convention in use.

North	South
(♠) A K 9 2	Q 10 6 3
(♥) K 8 6	A 9 7 2
(♦) A J 4 2	10 9 8
(♣) Q 2	K 5

With 17 points North has a strong one no-trump opening bid, and with nine points, plus two 10s, South has the values to raise to game. Still, if North holds four hearts or four spades a game will be easier in one of those suits, so South bids a Stayman two clubs. North responds two spades as he has four cards in the suit, and South raises to game in spades. Note that game in no-trumps is unlikely to succeed as a club lead will result in the declarer losing four club tricks and one outside trick.

Two no-trumps opening bid

This bid is always strong, showing 20–22 points and even distribution. Bid two no-trumps if you have the following hands:

(♠) A Q 2	K 10 2	Q J 10 6	K J
(♥) K Q 6 4	A 5	A K Q	A Q J 2
(♦) A 9 2	A Q 9 8	K 9 8	Q J 10
(♣) K Q 7	A K 6 2	A Q J	A K 8 6

Responses to an opening two no-trump bid

Again, a balanced or unbalanced hand governs the partner's reply. The response is quite simple. The opening bidder having shown 22 points for his bid needs only about four points from his partner. Generally with less than four points partner will pass unless he has a six-card suit or longer with a singleton or void. With four or more points and a balanced distribution, respond in no-trumps. With 11 points or more there is a possibility of a slam.

Partner has opened the bidding with no-trumps. What is the response holding?

Hand	Combined point count	Call
(a) (♠) 9 8 3 (♥) K 5 4 2 (♦) 7 6 5 (♣) 8 4 3	23 to 25	Pass

Comments: only in the event of a maximum hand can a game be envisaged.

| (b) (♠) 9 8 3
(♥) Q 9 8 6 5 4 2
(♦) –
(♣) 8 4 3 | 25 | Three hearts |

Comments: very unbalanced hand with fewer than four points. If partner bids three no-trumps, return to four hearts.

| (c) (♠) 9 8 3
(♥) K 9 8 6 5
(♦) 3 4
(♣) J 4 3 | 27 | Three hearts |

Comments: the comments for the previous hand apply here also.

| (d) (♠) 9 8 3
(♥) K 5 4 2
(♦) 7 6 5
(♣) Q 4 3 | 27 | Three no-trumps |

Comments: sufficient support to raise three no-trumps.

| (e) (♠) Q J 3
(♥) A K 4 2
(♦) 7 6 5
(♣) Q 10 4 | 36 | Six no-trumps |

Comments: partner should be able to make 12 tricks.

| (f) (♠) 5 3
(♥) K Q J 5 3
(♦) K Q 8
(♣) K 8 3 | 36 | Three hearts or
three clubs
Stayman |

Comments: if partner responds three no-trumps, raise to six. If partner responds four hearts, raise to six hearts.

Opening two club bids

There are some hands which are so strong that a game can be made with little or no help from partner. To tell your partner that you have a hand of this type you must open the bidding with the artificial bid of two clubs, even if you are void in that suit. This is known as a 'forcing to game' bid and your partner must keep the bidding open until game is reached (or the opponents have been doubled).

Here are some examples of two-club bids.

(♠) A K J 10 4	4 2	A K 10 6 5
(♥) A K J 6	A K Q J 10	A Q
(♦) A K 8 6	A K Q	K Q J
(♣) –	A Q J	A K 9

(♠) A K J 10 9 6	7 3	7 4 2
(♥) 8 5	A K Q J 4 2	6
(♦) A K 5	A K J 4	A K Q 8 6 4 2
(♣) K 6	7	A K

Response to a two club opening bid

If you have a hand containing no ace and no king you should respond two diamonds. This has the merit of keeping the bidding low so that your partner can show you the distribution of his hand as the bidding progresses. With an ace and a king, two king-queens, or three kings you should make a positive response. If you have a five-card suit or longer you should bid that suit, but if you have a balanced hand – that is a 4–3–3–3 distribution – you should respond two no-trumps.

Opening 'two' bids other than two clubs

This bid is not as strong as the opening two club and is only forcing for one round. It should be used for hands containing an excellent suit or suits and guarantees about eight playing tricks. On the left are some examples of opening 'two' bids other than two clubs.

Responses to bids of two in a suit other than two clubs

With a balanced hand and seven points or less the response should be two no-trumps. Should the opener re-bid his suit you are allowed to pass. If he re-bids another suit you can also pass unless he has made a jump bid, which again becomes forcing for one round. If you have a fair suit of your own with about nine or 10 points, you should bid this suit. If you make a positive response to an opening 'two' bid this is forcing to game.

Pre-emptive bidding

Opening bids of three or four in a suit are known as **pre-emptive** or **shut-out** bids. They are made with weak hands containing at least a seven-card suit and with little defensive value. They are designed to hamper the opponents and make it difficult for them to reach their best contract. However, you must have sufficient playing tricks so that if

you are doubled the loss will be no more than 500 points, i.e. three down if you are not vulnerable and two down if you are vulnerable.

Here are three examples of opening pre-emptive bids.

(a) (♠) x x
   (♥) K Q J 10 x x x x
   (♦) x
   (♣) x x

(b) (♠) Q J 10 9 x x x
   (♥) x x
   (♦) J 10 9 x
   (♣) –

(c) (♠) x
   (♥) K Q J x x x x
   (♦) x x
   (♣) Q J 10

Hand (a): you will be able to win seven tricks with hearts as trumps. If you are not vulnerable you will open the bidding with four hearts, so contracting for 10 tricks. If you are doubled and your partner has no tricks you will only incur a penalty of 500, less 100 for your honours. Had you been vulnerable you would have opened

with three hearts which contract, when doubled and two down, would have cost you 500 points, less the 100 honours.

Hand (b): you have five winning spade tricks and a diamond trick. If you are not vulnerable an opening three spade bid is correct. If you are vulnerable you must pass.

Hand (c): there are seven winners, six in hearts and one in clubs. If not vulnerable, bid four hearts; but if vulnerable bid only three.

Here are three more examples of pre-emptive bids, this time in the minor suits.

(a) (♠) x
   (♥) –
   (♦) K Q J x x x x x
   (♣) J 10 9 x

(b) (♠) –
   (♥) x x
   (♦) Q J 10 9
   (♣) Q J 10 x x x x

(c) (♠) x x
   (♥) x x
   (♦) x x
   (♣) K Q J 10 x x x

Hand (a): you have eight winners so if not vulnerable open five diamonds. If vulnerable bid four diamonds.

Hand (b): you have seven winners. If not vulnerable bid four clubs but if vulnerable bid only three clubs.

Hand (c): you have six winners. If not vulnerable bid three clubs but if vulnerable pass.

Partner's response to pre-emptive bids

These are quite simple to make. Whenever your partner makes a pre-emptive bid of three or four, you know he is overbidding his hand by two tricks if vulnerable and by three tricks if not vulnerable.

For example, if I, as your partner, opened the bidding when vulnerable with a bid of three spades and your hand was:

(♠) x x
(♥) A K x x
(♦) x x x x
(♣) x x x

. . . you would pass. I must be two winning tricks short of my bid which makes seven winners in my hand, and you have two tricks, thus making only nine instead of the 10 needed for a game in spades.

However, if your hand was

(♠) x x
(♥) A K x x
(♦) x x x x
(♣) A x x

. . . you would in this case raise me four spades.

Suppose however that I had opened the bidding when not vulnerable and you had either of these hands.

(a) (♠) x x
    (♥) A K x x
    (♦) x x x x
    (♣) x x x
(b) (♠) x x
    (♥) A K x x
    (♦) x x x x
    (♣) A x x

Hand (a): you would of course pass, knowing that when I bid three spades I was three tricks short of my contract.

Hand (b): you would also pass. The three winning tricks which you have are the three which were lacking when I opened three spades.

Opposing a pre-emptive bid

When you have a good hand and an opponent opens with a pre-emptive bid, you must exercise caution. With a good suit of your own there is no problem.

Holding:

(♠) A J x
(♥) A Q J 10 x x
(♦) A x
(♣) x x

. . . you will bid three hearts over an enemy bid of three clubs or three diamonds.

Holding a good hand but with no long suit there is a widely used convention which asks your partner to bid his best suit: that is a bid of three no-trumps.

A take-out bid of three no-trumps is similar to a take-out double. Therefore when your partner responds he should bid the full limit of his hand otherwise you will not know whether he has a good or a bad hand.

For example, if the bidding goes as follows:

South	West	North	East
3S	3NT	No	?

... with this hand:

(♠) x x x
(♥) x
(♦) K x x x x x
(♣) A K x

... East should respond five diamonds and not four. Opposite a take-out bid of three no-trumps this hand is good enough to bid a game.

If the bidding has gone:

South	West	North	East
3C	3NT	No	?

... and your hand is:

(♠) K x x
(♥) Q J 10 x
(♦) K 10 x
(♣) x x x

... over three no-trumps you should bid four hearts.

One important point to remember is that when an opponent pre-empts, you should be on the alert to try for a penalty rather than a doubtful game. Holding a hand such as:

(♠) A K x
(♥) Q J x x
(♦) K x
(♣) A J x x

... over a pre-emptive bid of three hearts or three diamonds you should double rather than bid three no-trumps.

'Forcing take-out'

A forcing take-out bid is a jump bid of one more than is necessary in a new suit. This bid is unconditionally forcing and the responder must keep the bidding open until a game is reached. If, after an initial call of one heart, the responder calls 'two spades', the bidding must not stop until a game has been reached. The jump response to one club is two diamonds; to one diamond, three clubs; to one heart, two spades; and to one spade, three hearts.

A 'triple raise'

A triple raise is a call of two more than is necessary. One heart/four hearts is an example and is a fairly strong call promising good support for partner's bid suit. Declarer should pass with a reasonable opening bid. A call of one heart/three spades, while still being a triple raise, is not a strong bid and is not forcing. It denotes a long suit and a wish to play the hand in that suit.

The re-bid by the opening bidder

The re-bid made by the opening bidder will obviously depend on the strength of his hand. With a holding of 13 to 16 points he must make a minimum re-bid: either one no-trump, two of his original call, or two of his partner's suit (if that suit was bid at the 'one' level).

With a holding of 17 to 19 points he will make a strong re-bid of two no-trumps, three of his original suit or three of his partner's suit. With 20 or more points he will either jump to three no-trumps, raise his partner's suit to game or make a jump bid in a new suit. Here are some examples.

The opening bidder has bid one heart and the responding hand has bid one spade. These are the re-bids that the opening bidder should now make.

Hand	Point value	Type of re-bid	Call
(a) (♠) J 3 (♥) A Q J 8 (♦) A 7 6 (♣) K 7 5 4	15	Minimum	One no-trump
(b) (♠) 8 3 (♥) A Q J 8 4 (♦) A 7 3 (♣) K 7 5	14	Minimum	Two hearts
Comments: original suit re-biddable			
(c) (♠) 8 6 5 3 (♥) A Q J 8 (♦) A 7 (♣) K 5 4	14	Minimum	Two spades
Comments: original suit not re-biddable; adequate trump support			
(d) (♠) 8 3 (♥) A Q J 8 (♦) A Q 3 (♣) K Q 5 4	18	Strong	Two no-trumps
Comments: shows strength in diamonds and clubs			
(e) (♠) 8 3 (♥) A K J 8 5 2 (♦) A 6 (♣) A 7 4	16	Strong	Three hearts
Comments: re-biddable suit in hearts			

Hand	Point value	Type of re-bid	Call
(f) (♠) 8 6 5 3 (♥) A Q J 8 (♦) A 7 (♣) A K 4	18	Strong	Four spades
Comments: adequate support in partner's suit			
(g) (♠) Q 3 (♥) A Q J 8 (♦) A Q 2 (♣) A 5 4 2	19	Very strong	Three no-trumps
Comments: game contract			
(h) (♠) K J 7 3 (♥) A Q J 8 (♦) 2 (♣) A K 5 4	18	Very strong	Four spades
Comments: jump bid to game			

Examples of opening bidder's re-bid when partner has responded either one no-trump or two of his suit:

Hand	Call	Comments
(a) (♠) A K 5 3 2 (♥) Q 6 5 (♦) A 5 4 (♣) 7 4	Pass	The hand is just an opening bid with no added values
(b) (♠) A K 6 5 3 2 (♥) Q 6 5 (♦) A 5 4 (♣) 7	Three spades	Though the hand has the same point count as the previous hand, the six-card spade suit makes it stronger. It has more trick-taking values
(c) (♠) A K 6 5 3 2 (♥) A 6 5 (♦) A Q 4 (♣) 7	Four spades	Additional help from partner not needed
(d) (♠) A K 5 3 2 (♥) Q 6 5 (♦) A 6 4 (♣) K 7	Two no-trumps	Asking partner to bid three if he has a maximum single raise

Responding hand's re-bid

Examples of responding hands re-bid after opener's second bid:

(a) South has opened one heart and North has responded one spade. South has then re-bid two diamonds. What should North bid with the hand opposite?

(b) South has opened one heart and North has responded one spade. South has then bid two spades. What should North respond with the hand opposite?

(c) South has opened one heart and North has responded one spade. South has then bid two spades. What should North respond with the hand opposite?

Hand (a)	Call	Comments
(♠) A 10 9 8 5 3 2 (♥) 6 (♦) 9 7 (♣) 10 9 4	Two spades	You have a simple re-bid

Hand (b)	Call	Comments
(♠) A 10 8 5 3 (♥) 6 4 (♦) 9 7 3 (♣) Q 9 4	No bid	Unlikely to make a game

Hand (c)	Call	Comments
(♠) A 10 9 8 5 3 2 (♥) 6 (♦) 9 7 (♣) 10 9 4	Four spades	Partner has raised spades and a game is probable in spite of the lack of points. The distribution is powerful enough to take the chance of going straight to game

Note that this hand is the same as hand (a), but in that case partner did not support spades but re-bid two diamonds.

(d) South has opened one heart and North has responded one spade. South has then bid two diamonds. What should North respond with the hand opposite?

Hand	Call	Comments
(♠) A 10 8 5 3 (♥) Q 9 6 4 (♦) K 3 (♣) 9 4	Three hearts	Too good for two hearts. Game is likely if partner has a good opening bid. This bid is not forcing

(e) South has opened one heart and North has responded one spade. South re-bids two diamonds. What should North respond with the hand opposite?

Hand	Call	Comments
(♠) A 10 9 8 3 (♥) K 3 (♦) 6 3 (♣) Q J 9 4	Two no-trumps	Enough points to make a game try

Bidding for a slam

Although there are many ways of reaching a slam, only two are described in this book: direct slam bidding; and the Blackwood Convention. Neither should be used unless you are fairly certain that the two hands can make the twelve tricks necessary for a little slam or the thirteen tricks needed for a grand slam. To make a small slam in no-trumps, or with an evenly balanced hand in a suit contract, you need a combined point count of at least 33. For a grand slam about 37 points are required.

Direct slam bidding

If the opening bidder has a strong hand and is given sufficient support by his partner, bid for a slam without delay. Let us consider this example.

The bidding has gone:

South	West	North	East
1S	No	3S	No

What should South bid holding:

Hand	Call	Comments
(♠) A Q J 9 5 (♥) A 3 (♦) A 5 2 (♣) K Q 7	Six spades	The combined hands should be able to make 12 tricks

The Blackwood Convention

The second way of reaching a slam is by the use of the **Blackwood Convention**. Should you and your partner agree to play this convention you must announce the fact to your opponents at the start of the rubber.

The Blackwood Convention is a method of finding out how many aces and kings are held by your partner. It is only used when the suit in which the final contract will be played has been agreed by the partnership. It is introduced by a bid of four no-trumps to which partner must reply. The replies which he can use are as follows:

Partner's bid	Response
Four no-trumps	With no ace respond five clubs With one ace respond five diamonds With two aces respond five hearts With three aces respond five spades With four aces respond five no-trumps

After the response to four no-trumps has been made, the initiator of that bid, if he thinks that a grand slam is possible, can now ask his partner for the number of kings that he holds. He bids five no-trumps and the replies are:

Partner's bid	Response
Five no-trumps	With no king respond six clubs With one king respond six diamonds With two kings respond six hearts With three kings respond six spades With four kings respond six no-trumps

These bids of four and five no-trumps are unconditionally forcing, and partner must not pass but should give the correct replies no matter how weak his hand might be.

Here is an example of the Blackwood Convention.

(♠) A K 10 6 4 2
(♥) A 5
(♦) Q 8 2
(♣) K 8

Your partner has responded three spades to your opening bid of one spade. It is essential to find out how many aces he holds. If partner responds five diamonds, sign off in five spades; but if he responds five hearts (two aces) bid six spades.

Playing the hand

Trick value of a card

The trick-winning value of a hand is estimated by the number of honour cards held and the length in each suit. In the section on bidding it was shown how the value of a hand can be assessed. When a hand is being played the trick-winning value of each card remaining in the hand changes as play proceeds. When the ace of a suit has been played the king then becomes the highest card in that suit. After the king, the queen, then the jack, and so on.

The player must train himself to remember which cards have been played in each suit and which cards remain to be played. This is not too difficult as each player can see the cards in his own hand and the cards in dummy. He has then only to remember the cards in the other two hands.

To the declarer falls the task of playing two hands, his own and the dummy. By the rules of the game, if he wins a trick from his own hand he must lead to the next trick from his own hand; if he wins a trick in the dummy he must play to the next trick from the dummy.

To release the trick-winning value of the cards held in the two hands the declarer must think ahead to the next and subsequent tricks. Here is a simple example. How does the declarer make three tricks out of these cards?

Dummy   (♥) A Q 2
Declarer   (♥) K 3

If the lead is in dummy the correct play is: first trick, play the (♥)2 and win with the (♥) king in own hand. Then play the (♥)3 and win in dummy with the (♥) ace. At the third trick play the (♥) queen from dummy and discard from own hand.

Dummy   (♥) A Q 2
Declarer   (♥) K J 3

In the second example (above), before playing his three tricks declarer must decide in which hand he wishes to finish. First trick: play the ace from dummy and the 3 from own hand.

Second trick: play the queen from dummy and own jack. Third trick: lead the 2 from dummy and take with the king. He now finishes in his own hand.

Dummy   (♥) Q 2
Declarer   (♥) K J 3

In the example above only two tricks can be made in the suit as the ace will take one trick. The proper play is to lead the queen from dummy.

Dummy   (♥) Q 2
Declarer   (♥) A K 6 4 3

In the example above take the first trick with dummy's queen and then play the cards in descending order.

The finesse

A **finesse** is an attempt to capture a trick with a card that is not the highest ranking in that suit.

```
              North (dummy)
              (♥) 6 3

West                          East
7 5                           K 4

              South
              A Q
```

In the example above it is dummy's turn to lead. If East follows with the king, South wins with the ace. If East plays the four, South plays the queen. As West does not hold the king, South's queen wins. This is known as **taking a finesse**.

Ruffing

Trumping a losing trick in one hand with a trump from the other is known as **ruffing**. Here is a situation which commonly arises.

Dummy   Declarer
(♠) A 10 9   (♠) 6
(♥) 5 3   (♥) A K 9 8

How many tricks can be made by the declarer if hearts are trumps? The (♥) A and K are sure winners, as is the (♠) A. When the lead is in dummy with the (♠) A, the (♠) 10 should be led and ruffed with the (♥) 9. Thus there are four tricks to be won with the five cards.

Planning the complete hand

When the bidding has finished and the opening player has led to the first trick, dummy places his hand face upwards on the table. The declarer should now take stock of the situation and plan how he is going to play the hand.

Playing the hand in no-trumps

Count the number of tricks that the combined hands can win in top cards and make your contract straight away. No-trump play is quite different from suit play. When you have a trump suit, your high and low cards in that suit are effective to prevent the opponents from winning tricks in their suit. In a no-trump contract you have only your high cards as a protection, so be sure you have a guard in every suit otherwise your opponents, who have the advantage of the lead, will attack in the suit in which you have no protection.

Here is an example (*see* top of next column). South to play in three no-trumps after the opening lead of the (♠) K by West. South must take the first trick with (♠) A and then make his four diamond tricks and his five club tricks, thus making ten tricks. He must on no account play a heart, or West will take his ace and cash his four winning spades to put the contract one down.

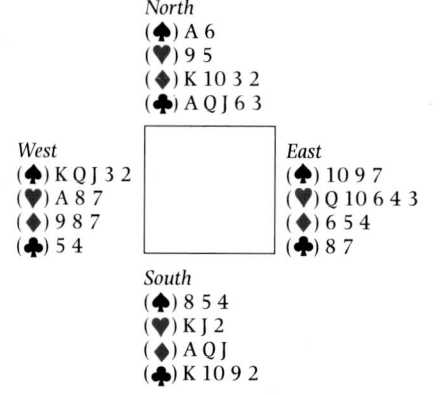

North
(♠) A 6
(♥) 9 5
(♦) K 10 3 2
(♣) A Q J 6 3

West
(♠) K Q J 3 2
(♥) A 8 7
(♦) 9 8 7
(♣) 5 4

East
(♠) 10 9 7
(♥) Q 10 6 4 3
(♦) 6 5 4
(♣) 8 7

South
(♠) 8 5 4
(♥) K J 2
(♦) A Q J
(♣) K 10 9 2

Hold-up play

In the next example (below) South, playing in three no-trumps, must not take the opening trick but must hold up his ace until the third round, thus preventing West from making his winning trick.

West leads the (♠) K against three no-trumps. South must not take the first or the second spade trick. He must take the ace on the third round followed by the diamond finesse. When East wins with

his (♦) K he cannot return to a spade. South thus makes his contract with one spade trick, four diamond tricks, three club tricks and two heart tricks.

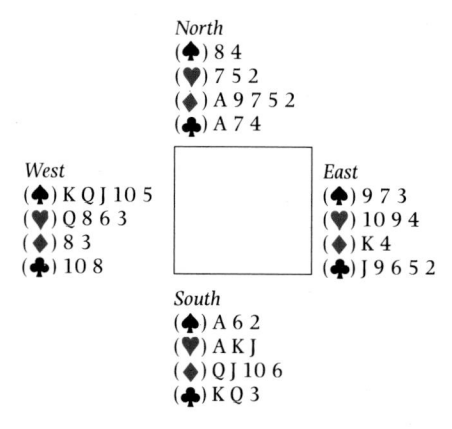

North
(♠) 8 4
(♥) 7 5 2
(♦) A 9 7 5 2
(♣) A 7 4

West
(♠) K Q J 10 5
(♥) Q 8 6 3
(♦) 8 3
(♣) 10 8

East
(♠) 9 7 3
(♥) 10 9 4
(♦) K 4
(♣) J 9 6 5 2

South
(♠) A 6 2
(♥) A K J
(♦) Q J 10 6
(♣) K Q 3

In no-trumps play the declarer must always try to establish his longest suit, either in his hand or in the dummy. For example, if his holding in clubs and spades is (♠) K Q J 10, (♠) K Q J 10 9, he must attack the clubs first. As the opponents hold both these aces, if the declarer first plays the clubs he will be able to take four tricks in that suit but only three in the spade suit.

When the declarer and the dummy have the same number of cards in each suit, for example:

Dummy
(♠) Q J 10 8
(♦) Q J 10 6 3
Declarer
(♠) K 6 4 2
(♦) K 9 5

... he should attack the longer suit first. In this case he must knock out the (♦) A as that suit will yield four tricks.

Declarer's play of suit contracts

Normally, when you are playing in a suit contract you draw the trumps and then proceed to make your winning tricks in the side suits. But when you have an unbalanced hand with either a void or a singleton you should not play any trumps but utilise them to ruff losers in either hand. The following hand (*see top of next column*) is an example of when *not* to draw trumps.

South is playing in four hearts. West leads the (♦) A, K and a small one, and South wins with his queen. If you now draw the trumps you will have to lose at least two spade tricks and will not be able to make your contract. You must now play your singleton club to dummy's ace, a spade from dummy to your ace, ruff a spade in dummy, ruff a club in your hand, ruff a third spade in dummy, play off your (♥) K, return to your hand with a club – ruffing higher than East if he ruffs first – draw the remainder of the trumps and make your contract. The only tricks that you have lost are the (♦) A and K.

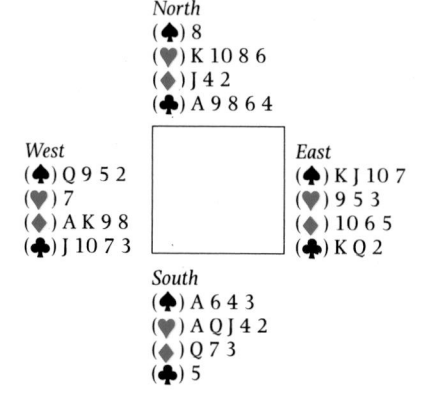

North
(♠) 8
(♥) K 10 8 6
(♦) J 4 2
(♣) A 9 8 6 4

West
(♠) Q 9 5 2
(♥) 7
(♦) A K 9 8
(♣) J 10 7 3

East
(♠) K J 10 7
(♥) 9 5 3
(♦) 10 6 5
(♣) K Q 2

South
(♠) A 6 4 3
(♥) A Q J 4 2
(♦) Q 7 3
(♣) 5

Discarding losers on winners

You are South playing the following hand in a contract of four spades. The opening lead is the (♦) K. The defenders take their (♦) A, K and Q and then lead a heart. You now have two heart losers. You take your (♥) A, and after drawing the trumps discard them on the clubs, thus making five spade tricks, four club tricks and the (♥) A for your game.

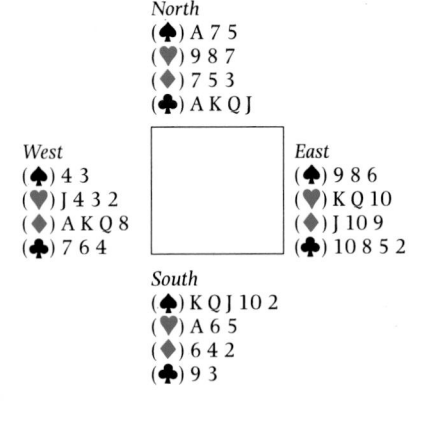

North
(♠) A 7 5
(♥) 9 8 7
(♦) 7 5 3
(♣) A K Q J

West
(♠) 4 3
(♥) J 4 3 2
(♦) A K Q 8
(♣) 7 6 4

East
(♠) 9 8 6
(♥) K Q 10
(♦) J 10 9
(♣) 10 8 5 2

South
(♠) K Q J 10 2
(♥) A 6 5
(♦) 6 4 2
(♣) 9 3

Establishing winners for discards

You are playing the following hand in four spades. You have three heart losers and one diamond so you must try to establish an extra club trick to dispose of your losing diamond.

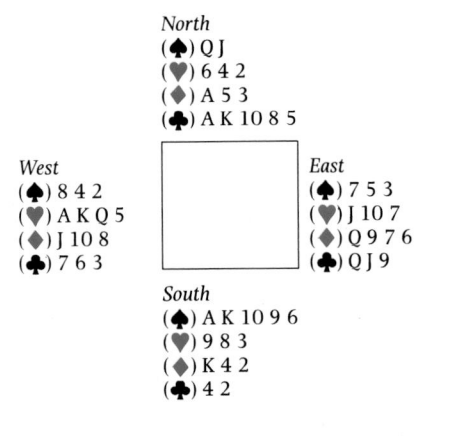

North
(♠) Q J
(♥) 6 4 2
(♦) A 5 3
(♣) A K 10 8 5

West
(♠) 8 4 2
(♥) A K Q 5
(♦) J 10 8
(♣) 7 6 3

East
(♠) 7 5 3
(♥) J 10 7
(♦) Q 9 7 6
(♣) Q J 9

South
(♠) A K 10 9 6
(♥) 9 8 3
(♦) K 4 2
(♣) 4 2

West leads the (♥) A, K and Q followed by a diamond. It is very important that you take this trick in your hand and not in the dummy as you will need dummy's ace for a re-entry later

on. You now play off the queen and jack of trumps and the (♣) A and K, followed by a third club which you must ruff in your hand with a high trump in case West has no more clubs. You now must draw the last two trumps and then enter dummy with the (♦) A to discard your losing diamond on the (♣) 10 which is now a master card.

The following hand is slightly more difficult and needs a little more reflection. The contract is three no-trumps by South, and West leads the (♠) 3.

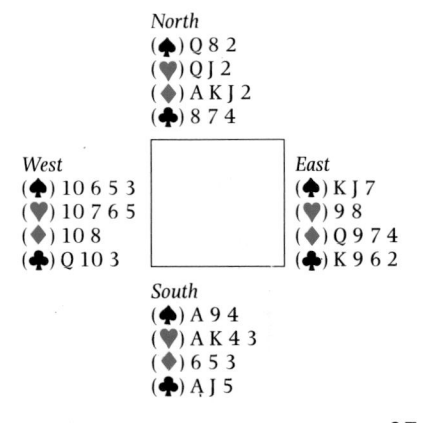

North
(♠) Q 8 2
(♥) Q J 2
(♦) A K J 2
(♣) 8 7 4

West
(♠) 10 6 5 3
(♥) 10 7 6 5
(♦) 10 8
(♣) Q 10 3

East
(♠) K J 7
(♥) 9 8
(♦) Q 9 7 4
(♣) K 9 6 2

South
(♠) A 9 4
(♥) A K 4 3
(♦) 6 5 3
(♣) A J 5

South can count eight tricks, and nine if the diamond finesse is right. But when the (♠) 3 is led and East plays the jack, South can now see his ninth trick. The play of the (♠) J tells the declarer that East does not hold the 10, as when you are defending a contract you always play the lower of two touching cards provided that you are not on lead. The 10, therefore, should be with West, so now you can play your (♠) 4 and lead up to dummy's queen and eight. If West plays low, you finesse the eight, and if East has the king then your queen becomes a master card in the dummy. If West has both the king and the 10 then your eight takes the trick and gives you your ninth trick for your game. Although East may be bluffing with his play of the jack, the play offers a better chance than a direct diamond finesse. This can always be tried later if the spade play fails.

Defending

The game of bridge is such that all the advantage is not necessarily with the attacking side; good play by the defenders often results in their collecting points which an attacking side has lost through weak play.

Opening leads

The most difficult moment for the defenders is the opening lead. It so often makes all the difference between the declarer making his contract or going down. Some information is obtained by the opening leader during the auction, but he only sees his own hands so has to make a difficult choice as to which card to lead. The first thing to consider is whether the contract is being played in a suit or in no-trumps. Unfortunately, in bridge you cannot lay down exact rules and say 'always lead this' or 'never lead that'. Not even the experts are right all the time; only more often than the average player.

The following are leads which are in general use.

● Lead the suit which your partner has bid. If you have three or four to an honour lead the lowest one, otherwise lead the top card in the suit. This is known as a **directed lead**, because when your partner has made either an opening bid or an overbid he will presumably have tricks in the suit.

● Lead from a sequence of three or more touching honours. K Q J 10 x; or Q J 10 x x; or Q J 10. When you lead the king and it is taken by the opponent's ace you will have established two tricks in the suit.

● Lead the fourth best of your suit. This follows the 'rule of eleven' detailed shortly.

● Lead a singleton or a doubleton.

Defending against no-trump contracts

Against no-trump contracts it is essential to try to develop winning tricks out of the smaller cards, so you must lead your longest suit. For example, you hold:

(♠) 8 5 3
(♥) A J 10
(♦) A 9
(♣) Q J 8 6 3

Your lead against a no-trump contract is your fourth highest which is the (♣) 6. Had your club suit been Q, J, 10, 6, 3, you should have selected the queen. In any situation where three touching honours are held, the highest takes the place of the fourth best.

The 'rule of eleven'

We have just seen that when you are making a lead from a long suit you should lead your fourth highest. This is called the **rule of eleven**. It works like this. When your partner leads a card, you subtract the number of that card from eleven. You then take away from the dummy any cards that are higher than the resulting number, and finally subtract your own higher cards. The answer will tell you just how many cards higher than the opening lead are in the declarer's hand. To give you an example:

Dummy	(♥) K 10 8 5
West leads the	(♥) 6
You have	(♥) Q 9 2

Take six from 11, which leaves five, three from the dummy (K, 10 and 8), two from your hand (Q and 9) and now there are none left, so declarer has no card higher than the 6. Therefore on the (♥) 5 from the dummy you merely play your 2. If declarer plays the 8 you merely cover with the 9. Here is a second example:

Dummy	(♠) J 6
West leads the	(♠) 5
You have	(♠) A 9 4

Five from 11 equals six; two from six equals four; two from four equals two. You now know that the declarer has two cards higher than the 5.

This lead, while sometimes aiding the declarer, is of use to your partner on the majority of occasions.

As we have seen, whenever possible you should lead the fourth highest of your longest suit. Sometimes, however, this suit has already been bid by the declarer. When this happens you must make an alternative lead. And should you be forced from A x x or K x x you should lead the smallest one. Your partner may be deceived but will realise that you have at least one honour.

A doubleton lead against no-trumps is not a good one, and a singleton should rarely be led.

Below are some examples of the correct opening lead against no-trump contracts, where touching honours are held.

Holding in suit	Lead	Holding in suit	Lead
A K Q J x x	A	J 10 9 x x	J
A K x	K	A Q J 10 x	Q
K Q J x	K	A Q 10 9 x	10
Q J 10 x	Q	K J 10 5 x	J
Q J 9 8	Q	Q 10 9 x x	10

Defending against suit contracts

On many occasions you will have a difficult problem. Suppose, for instance, your partner has not bid and your best suit has been bid by your opponents. You have been warned, so you must find a different lead. You now may lead from a doubleton, for that offers a better prospect of making a trick as you may be able to trump the third round. For example:

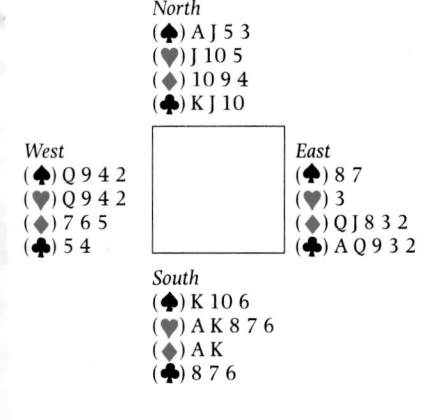

North
(♠) A J 5 3
(♥) J 10 5
(♦) 10 9 4
(♣) K J 10

West
(♠) Q 9 4 2
(♥) Q 9 4 2
(♦) 7 6 5
(♣) 5 4

East
(♠) 8 7
(♥) 3
(♦) Q J 8 3 2
(♣) A Q 9 3 2

South
(♠) K 10 6
(♥) A K 8 7 6
(♦) A K
(♣) 8 7 6

South is playing in four hearts. After North's original response of one spade West has to find a lead. As both spades and hearts have been bid, West can now play from his doubleton club which gives a better attacking prospect than the trebleton diamond. His partner takes the ace and the queen and gives him a ruff on the third round. West then must make his queen of hearts to defeat the contract.

When you have elected to lead from a doubleton or a worthless trebleton you must lead the highest. This lead is called the **top of nothing** lead.

The lead of a singleton against a suit contract may also turn out to be a good lead. If your partner has the ace of that suit he will take the trick and return it for you to make a trump. Should you be able to give him the lead again before the trumps are drawn you will be able to make a second trump trick.

(♠) A Q 7 4 2
(♥) 6 4 2
(♦) 7
(♣) 9 6 4 2

With this hand the best lead against a four-heart contract would be the single-

ton diamond, even though you have a five-card suit.

The opening lead of a trump:

(♠) A J 9 7
(♥) 9 8 4
(♦) K 10 9
(♣) K J 7

You should lead a trump against a suit contract when you do not want to lead any other suit in case you help the declarer. Here is a hand where a trump would be the best lead. The contract is four hearts.

There is also another occasion for leading trumps; that is when the declarer has bid two suits and you have tricks in his second suit.

This is illustrated by the following hand.

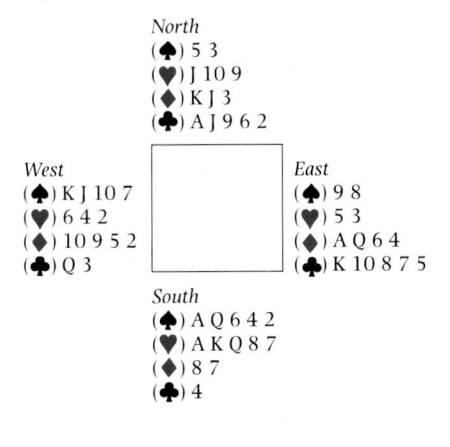

North
(♠) 5 3
(♥) J 10 9
(♦) K J 3
(♣) A J 9 6 2

West
(♠) K J 10 7
(♥) 6 4 2
(♦) 10 9 5 2
(♣) Q 3

East
(♠) 9 8
(♥) 5 3
(♦) A Q 6 4
(♣) K 10 8 7 5

South
(♠) A Q 6 4 2
(♥) A K Q 8 7
(♦) 8 7
(♣) 4

South is the declarer in four hearts. He has bid both spades and hearts and you know that he has five of each. You should lead a trump and when you make your (♠) K you should lead a further trump. He will now have to lose two spades and two diamond tricks.

The proprieties

Players should be very careful to guard against any conduct which may give unfair information to their partner. All the calls should be made in the same tone of voice and a player would be guilty of reprehensible conduct if he allowed his partner's hesitation or remarks to influence him in a call, lead or play.

The good player should never nag or bully his less capable partner, but should try to keep on good terms with him throughout the rubber. He should not point out his partner's errors unless asked: 'Could I have made the contract, partner?'

Every player should study the Laws of Bridge, as ignorance of these can cause many unpleasant discussions. A copy of the rules should always be available in case it is needed.

Always remember that there is nothing worse than a bad loser, unless it is a gloating winner.

Tournament play – duplicate bridge

Enthusiasts who are keen to improve their game and progress will choose to compete in the duplicate bridge events regularly held in their local bridge clubs. Each hand is played by all the participants – hence 'duplicate'.

The cards are dealt and the hands placed in specially constructed boards or *wallets* which are played and passed on from table to table. Thus everybody plays the same hands under identical conditions. Special sheets on which the results are entered accompany the boards throughout. At the end the scorer 'match points' them and they are entered on a master sheet. From this each pair can see at a glance how they have performed in comparison with their competitors.

Although the scoring is different from that of rubber bridge, it is easily learnt and should not cause any difficulty. In general the basic elements in bidding and play are much the same.

The next step

When bridge players have mastered the basic essentials and gained more experience, they adopt additional refinements to their bidding and play in an effort to improve their game and suit their particular requirements.

A system known as **ACOL** is very popular and successful with the ordinary player, but there are other more involved systems usually adopted by more experienced players. An extensive library of books on the game exists, written by distinguished exponents. If you want to improve your bridge and broaden your outlook, a comprehensive study of the literature of the game cannot fail to help you.

Bridge is a wonderful game. It is well worthwhile devoting time and effort to learning it.

Scoring table

Trick points for: declarer

Each trick over six bid and won in:	Undoubled	Doubled	Re-doubled
clubs or diamonds	20	40	80
hearts or spades	30	60	120
no-trumps (first trick)	40	80	160
(each subsequent trick)	30	60	120

Vulnerability does not affect the trick score. 100 points are needed for a game.

Premium points for: defenders declarers

Over-tricks

	Not vulnerable	Vulnerable
Undoubled, each	trick value	trick value
Doubled, each	100	200
Bonus for making doubled contract	50	50

Under-tricks

	Not vulnerable	Vulnerable
Undoubled, each	50	100
Doubled: first trick	100	200
second trick	200	300
third trick	200	300
fourth and subsequent tricks	300	300

Re-doubling doubles the doubled points for over-tricks and under-tricks.

Premium points for: declarers holders (rubber bridge only)

	Not vulnerable	Vulnerable
Four honours in one hand	100	100
Five honours in one hand	150	150
Four aces in one hand (no-trumps only)	150	150
Little slam	500	750
Grand slam	1000	1500
Two game rubber	700	
Three game rubber	500	

Unfinished rubber: the winner of one game scores 300 points. If one side has a part score in an unfinished game it scores 100 points. Doubling or re-doubling does not affect honour, slam or rubber points. Vulnerability does not affect points for honours.

Glossary

Auction   The bidding.

Balanced hand   Hand with two or more cards in each suit.

Bid   To make a bid is to undertake to win a certain number of tricks in a named suit or in no-trumps.

Blackwood Convention   Method of discovering how many aces and kings are held by partner.

Book   First six tricks scored by a partnership.

Call   Four alternatives: pass, double, re-double, a bid.

Contract   Defined by the final call of the auction. Five possible denominations: no-trumps, spades, hearts, diamonds, clubs.

Convention   Special bid or play.

Cut   Draw for partners; dividing of pack before deal.

Deal   Dishing out the cards, face downwards and one at a time clockwise around the table, 13 to each player.

Declarer   The player who first names the suit in the contract and who thus plays the hand.

Discard   To play a no-trump when unable to follow suit.

Distribution   The way in which the cards are distributed in the suits, thus determining the shape and strength of the hand.

Double   To double the last bid made by an opponent.

Doubleton   Holding two cards in a suit.

Dummy   The declarer's partner whose cards are placed face-up on the table immediately after the opening lead.

Entries   Cards which allow the lead to move from one hand to the other – very important to good declarer play.

Finesse   Attempt to promote a lower ranking card when a higher one is held by an opponent.

Hold up   To decline to play a winning card on a trick.

Honour   One of the five highest cards in a suit – ace, king, queen, jack or 10.

Insufficient bid   A bid which is lower than the previous one.

Laws   These cover every aspect of the game. They supply a solution for every contingency, and should always be applied whenever the normal course of play is disturbed.

Lead   The first card played in a trick.

Little slam   Contract of six odd tricks bid and made.

Major suit   Spades or hearts.

Minor suit   Diamonds or clubs.

Non-vulnerable A side which has not won a game.

Odd tricks Tricks in addition to the book.

Opening bidder First player to bid in an auction.

Pass A call demonstrating reluctance to make a bid or to double or re-double.

Penalty Points scored above the line when an opponent has failed to make his contract.

Pre-emptive Opening bids of three or four in a suit.

Promote To increase the value of a card by removing the opponent's higher card.

Re-biddable suit Suit of such strength that it can be bid again by the same player later in the auction.

Raise Direct support for partner's bid.

Re-double To double a doubled contract.

Responder Partner of opening bidder.

Reverse bid A re-bid of a higher ranking suit than the one bid originally. Denotes strength.

Rubber Best of three games.

Ruffing Trumping a losing trick in one hand with a trump from the other.

Sacrifice bidding Aiming to deprive the opponents of a game or slam by making a bid that the player does not expect to make.

Sequence Two or more consecutive cards, usually high ranking in the suit.

Signalling Successful defence depends on partnership co-operation. By using signals, useful information can be exchanged between the defenders which will help to restrict the contract. The usual method is by means of a PETER – playing high-low in a suit. This shows your partner you have an interest in that suit and he can play to it when he next has the lead.

Singleton Holding one card in a suit.

Stayman Convention Used in response to an opening one no-trump bid in order to explore the possibilities of playing the hand in a major suit of which the partners hold at least four cards each in that suit.

Trick Four cards, one played by each player in rotation.

Triple raise A call of two more than is necessary.

Trump A card of the suit named in the final bid.

Void Having no cards in a suit in the original holding.

Vulnerable A side that has won a game, after which penalties and bonuses are increased.

Useful addresses

The British Bridge League
The Old Railway Station
Long Melford
Sudbury
Suffolk
CO10 9HN

The English Bridge Union
Broadfields
Bicester Road
Aylesbury
Buckinghamshire
HP19 3BG

The Scottish Bridge Union
32 Whitehaugh Drive
Paisley
PA1 3PG

The Welsh Bridge Union
19 Penygraig
Rhiwbina
Cardiff
CF4 6ST

The Northern Ireland Bridge Union
9 Upper Malone Road
Belfast
BT9 6TD

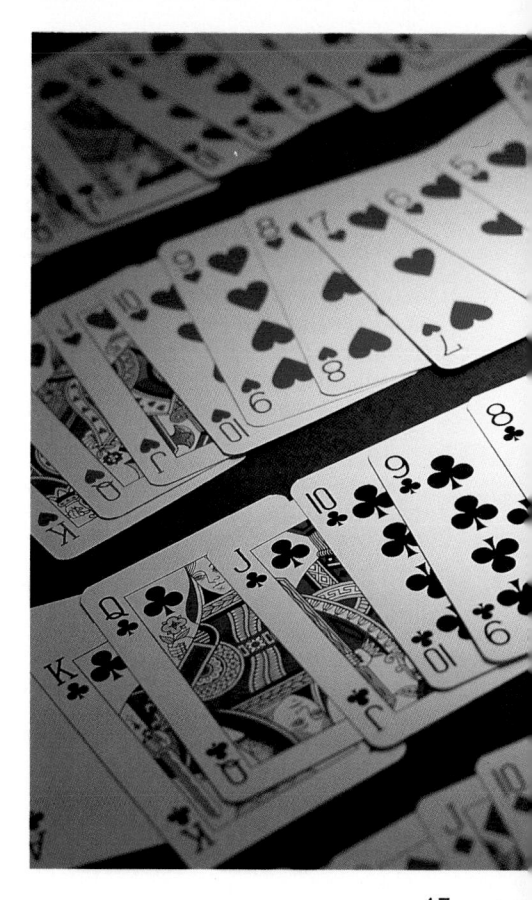

Index